My Grandpa Could do ANYTHING in Hawaii!

by Ric Dilz

Mahalo to all the Grandpas
in the world.

REINdesigns, inc.
Boulder, Colorado

Illustration & Design by Nancy Maysmith, Helen Harrison & Ric Dilz

My Grandpa could do ANYTHING...

My Grandpa
doesn't bungee jump
from a palm tree...

But he could!

My Grandpa
doesn't take first place
in a surfing contest...

But he could!

My Grandpa
doesn't do 100 push ups
with a gecko...

But he could!

My Grandpa
doesn't do tricks
on a paddle board...

But he could!

My Grandpa
doesn't play a ukulele
on a zip line...

But he could!

My Grandpa
doesn't fly a
helicopter around
a volcano...

But he could!

My Grandpa
doesn't juggle fire sticks
at a hula show...

But he could!

My Grandpa
doesn't kite surf
with a turtle...

But he could!

My Grandpa
doesn't swim as fast
as a yellowfin tuna...

But he could!

My Grandpa
doesn't spout water
like a whale...

But he could!

My Grandpa
doesn't race
spinner dolphins
to the mainland....

But he could!

My Grandpa
doesn't hang glide
off a cliff...

But he could!

My Grandpa
could do lots of things,
but I'm so happy with
the one thing he does
the best...

Can you find these Hawaii friends in this book

teardrop butterfly fish

sergeant major

yellow tang

'i'iwi

dolphin

humu

gecko

moorish idol

monk seal

sea turtle

yellowfin tuna

humpback whale

nēnē

octopus

Can you find the pictures that go with these Hawaiian words?

ahi—fire
`āina—land, earth
ānuenue—rainbow

hala kahiki—pineapple
hōkū—star
honu—turtle

kahakai—beach
koholā—humpback whale

keiki—Child or children; kids
kūkū—Grandpa

lei—garland of flowers, leaves,
    nuts, or shells
limu—seaweed

mahina—moon
makai—ocean, ocean water

mele—song
mauka—mountain
moku—island
moana—ocean, sea

nai'a—dolphin
nalu—wave
niu—coconut

pālama—palm tree
pali—cliff
pulelehua—butterfly

tūtū—Grandma

ukulele—stringed instrument,
    small guitar

wa`a—canoe
wai—water (not salt water)

 Did you find me, Tiki Turtle, in every picture?

Share more laughs with these fun books

Available at www.jibberjabbers.com/books

Published by Rein Designs, Inc. Boulder, Colorado

ISBN: 978-0-9859684-2-7

Library of Congress Control Number: 2014904708

Printed in China